3/07 dirty fingerprints thru page

MW01053629

Wild Turkeys

by Dorothy Hinshaw Patent
photographs by William Muñoz

Lerner Publications Company • Minneapolis, Minnesota

For my family
—DHP

For Joe and Sue
—WM

Thanks to our series consultant, Sharyn Fenwick, elementary science/math specialist. Mrs. Fenwick was the winner of the National Science Teachers Association 1991 Distinguished Teacher Award. She was also the recipient of the Presidential Award for Excellence in Math and Science Teaching, representing the state of Minnesota at the elementary level in 1992.

Early Bird Nature Books were conceptualized by Ruth Berman and designed by Steve Foley. Series editor is Joelle Goldman.

Website address: www.lernerbooks.com

Library of Congress Cataloging-in-Publication Data

Patent, Dorothy Hinshaw.
    Wild Turkeys / by Dorothy Hinshaw Patent ; photographs by William
Muñoz.
        p. cm. — (Early bird nature books)
    Includes index.
    Summary: Describes the physical characteristics, habitat,
behavior, and life cycle of wild turkeys.
    ISBN 0–8225–3026–0 (alk. paper)
    1. Wild turkey—Juvenile literature.   [1. Wild turkey.
2. Turkeys.]   I. Muñoz, William, ill. II. Title. III. Series.
QL696.G27P38 1999
598.6'45—dc21   98–20466

Manufactured in the United States of America
1 2 3 4 5 6 – SP – 04 03 02 01 00 99

Contents

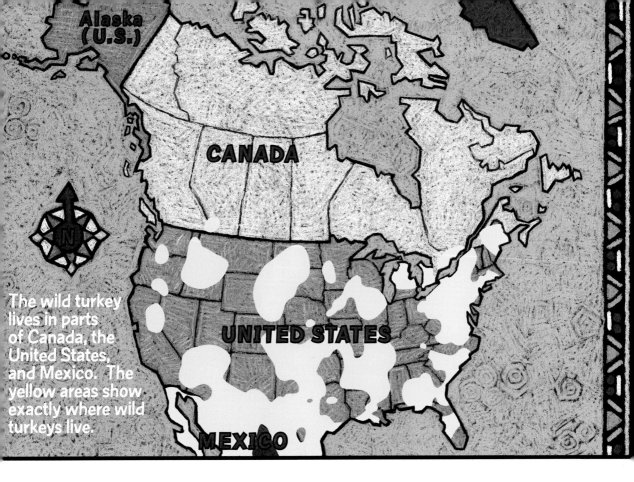

The wild turkey lives in parts of Canada, the United States, and Mexico. The yellow areas show exactly where wild turkeys live.

Be a Word Detective

Can you find these words as you read about the wild turkey's life? Be a detective and try to figure out what they mean. You can turn to the glossary on page 46 for help.

beard	gobblers	roosting
displaying	hens	snood
domesticated	incubating	spurs
down	poults	toms
flock	predators	

Chapter 1

In Thanksgiving pictures, turkeys are round. They have fluffy feathers and wide tails. Is this what all turkeys look like?

What Is a Turkey?

 We all know what turkeys are like.

Every fall we see pictures of fat turkeys with

wide tails. When we eat Thanksgiving dinner, we see the plump roasted bird on the platter. But are these real turkeys?

Turkeys don't always look like Thanksgiving turkeys. Wild turkeys usually look sleek and slim.

Yes, the bird on the dinner table is a turkey. But it isn't a wild one. The turkeys we eat have been raised on farms. They are domesticated (duh-MESS-tih-kay-tehd).

Domesticated turkeys' feathers may be red, brown, black, gray, or white. But most domesticated turkeys have white feathers.

Some turkey farms have huge flocks of domesticated turkeys.

Domesticated animals have been raised by people for a long time. They have become different from their wild relatives. Domesticated turkeys are specially grown to have large muscles. The muscles become tender meat for us to eat.

Domesticated turkeys have sturdy legs and a medium-sized neck. Their bodies are plump. Domesticated turkeys are so heavy that they can't fly once they are grown. Most domesticated turkeys have white feathers.

Wild turkeys have long, slender legs and a long neck. Their bodies are slim and sleek.

Domesticated turkeys have fat, round bodies. Fully grown domesticated turkeys cannot fly.

Wild turkeys have long, slim bodies and dark, shiny feathers. The scientific name of the wild turkey is Meleagris gallopavo.

Wild turkeys have strong wings that carry them easily into the air. They have beautiful dark feathers with many shiny colors.

People in many parts of the world raise domesticated turkeys. But wild turkeys live only in the United States, Canada, and Mexico. They live in woods and fields.

Chapter 2

A wild turkey is up to 4 feet long from its beak to the tip of its tail. How fast can a turkey run?

The Wild Turkey

Wild turkeys are big birds. Most males weigh more than 16 pounds. They are called toms or gobblers. The females, or hens, usually weigh about 9 pounds. A turkey can stand 4 feet tall. Its wings spread 5 to 6 feet from tip to tip when it flies.

A wild turkey can fly as fast as 50 miles per hour. That is about the speed of a fast racehorse. A wild turkey is fast even when it is not flying. It can run 25 miles an hour, as fast as a speedy human can run.

Wild turkeys don't fly often. But they can fly fast for short distances.

Toms and hens look different. Toms have lots of bare skin on their head and neck. Hens have just a little bare skin. Toms have a loose piece of skin above their beak. This piece of skin is called the snood. Hens don't have a snood.

Toms have only a few stubby feathers on their head and neck. The skin on a tom's head is usually pink or light blue.

Most of a hen's neck is covered with feathers.

Toms have a tuft of long, thin feathers growing from their chest. These long feathers are called a beard. A tom's beard can be 8 inches long. Hens don't usually have a beard. If they do, it is very short.

The tuft of thin, dark feathers hanging from this tom's chest is his beard. The rest of his chest feathers are shiny brown with black tips.

Toms have sharp spines called spurs on the backs of their legs. The spurs are used for fighting. Hens don't have spurs.

The feather tips on the tom's chest are black. The hen's feather tips are light tan. This makes female turkeys look lighter in color than males.

This hen doesn't have a beard hanging from her chest. Her chest feathers have light tan edges.

Turkeys spend the day looking for food. They eat many foods, such as berries, seeds, nuts, mushrooms, and insects. Turkeys use their strong feet to scratch at the ground for food.

Every evening as the sky darkens, turkeys fly up into the trees. This is called roosting.

Turkeys spend most of their time looking for food. One of their favorite foods is acorns.

It is hard for a predator to catch a turkey who is roosting in a tree. Bobcats and coyotes are two kinds of predators who hunt turkeys.

Birds roost at night to rest and sleep. In the trees, turkeys are safe from most animals that can hunt and eat them. These animals are called predators (PREH-duh-turz). The turkeys roost in the trees until dawn. Then they return to the ground to look for food.

Chapter 3

For most of the year, toms look sleek and slim. When do they puff up like Thanksgiving turkeys?

Starting a Family

Most of the time, wild turkeys look slim. But in the late winter and early spring, toms puff up their body feathers. They spread their tails into fans. Then they look like Thanksgiving turkeys. When toms do these things, they are displaying. Toms display to try to attract hens. When toms display, they make their special "gobble" call. Toms are the only turkeys who gobble.

Usually, most of the skin on a wild gobbler's head and neck is blue. But when he displays, some of it turns bright red. The tom's snood becomes big. It may turn red, too. It hangs down along one side of his beak.

Toms gobble when they display. The gobbling can be heard up to a mile away.

When toms display, they are showing off for hens. A displaying tom can quickly change his skin color from whitish blue to bright red.

When a tom displays, he tucks in his chin. He spreads his tail to show off his colorful feathers. He lowers his wings until the tips touch the ground. Then the tom takes a few quick steps toward the hen. He makes a soft "chunk" sound. His wings rustle as they drag on the ground. Then he turns so his tail feathers face the hen. The tom finishes his display with a gobble.

As spring fades, the toms join one another in small groups. The hens go off alone to start a family.

Wild toms are not the only turkeys who display.
Domesticated toms also display.

Chapter 4

Wild turkey hens hide their nests and their babies well. People seldom see them. What are wild turkeys' nests made of?

The Life of the Chicks

Each hen makes a nest of dry leaves on the ground. She makes her nest among the bushes in a forest. She chooses a spot that is near a meadow or clearing.

A turkey hen takes two weeks to lay 10 to 12 eggs. She sits on the eggs in the nest and keeps them warm. This is called incubating (ING-kyuh-bay-ting). When a bird incubates, a bare patch of warm skin on its chest touches the eggs. Without the warmth from the hen's body, the chick inside the egg would never grow.

This domesticated hen is sitting on her eggs. About four weeks after she has finished laying eggs, they will begin to hatch.

Turkeys' eggs are creamy white with brown speckles. They are much bigger than chickens' eggs.

By late May or early June, turkey eggs are ready to hatch. The chicks inside the eggs make soft peeping sounds. Their mother answers with quiet yelps. Each chick has a sharp egg tooth on the tip of its beak. The chick also has a special hatching muscle on the back of its head. Using the hatching muscle, the chick bangs its egg tooth on the inside of the eggshell. Bit by bit, the chick turns inside the egg. It slowly breaks a circle through the shell. Then the shell opens and the chick struggles out. The chick's egg tooth soon falls off, and the hatching muscle disappears.

Hatching is hard work. It takes two to three days for a chick to break out of its shell.

Turkey chicks are called poults (POHLTS). When they hatch, poults are covered with short feathers called down. The poults' feathers are wet at first, but they quickly dry out. The fluffy down feathers help keep the little poults warm.

These domesticated turkey poults have just hatched. Each poult has an egg tooth on the tip of its beak. The egg tooth looks like a tiny fingernail.

Young poults make soft peeping sounds.

The poults can walk right away. When all her poults have hatched, the mother turkey leaves the nest. She calls to the poults to follow her. The family heads to the nearby clearing to feed.

From the time they hatch, poults eat the same foods as adult turkeys eat.

The poults follow their mother closely. She can protect them from predators. At night, the hen roosts on the ground. She usually chooses a spot that is next to a tree. The poults snuggle together under her wings and body. They are safe there.

When the poults are just two weeks old, their adult feathers have started to grow. The poults can fly short distances. At night, they roost in trees with their mother.

These poults have begun to grow adult wing feathers.

Turkey poults grow quickly. Soon these young turkeys will be fully grown.

During the day, the poults look for food with their mother. If the hen notices a predator, she calls out with a sharp cry. The poults flutter up into the nearest tree. The mother flies

Wild turkeys can see well. They can hear much better than people can. Wild turkeys always watch and listen for danger.

farther away from the poults to confuse the predator. When the predator moves away, the poults peep for their mother. She comes back when the danger is over.

Chapter 5

In the summer, many families of wild turkeys come together to make a big group. What is a group of birds called?

Growing Up

As the poults grow, families of hens and poults join together to make flocks. A flock is a group of birds. There may be 50 turkeys in one flock. The flock travels far in search of food.

Some flocks have hens, poults, and toms. Other flocks are made up of only toms.

The young turkeys grow fast. By November, the young hens weigh 6 to 8 pounds. The tom poults are bigger. They weigh up to 13 pounds.

In the fall, turkeys have to travel a long way to find enough food.

Big flocks break up into small family groups in the fall. Small groups of turkeys do not need as much food as large groups.

As winter approaches, food becomes harder to find. The young birds grow more slowly. The big flocks break up into family groups once again. In winter, the birds do not roam very far. Cold weather and snow slow them down.

When spring comes, young turkeys leave their mothers. The hens are ready to start new families.

By springtime, the young hens are ready to start families. They are fully grown. But their brothers are not. It takes three years for a tom to grow his long beard.

Turkey hens usually live 6 to 9 years. Gobblers may live longer. Sometimes gobblers live to be 12 or even 14 years old.

Turkeys cluck to one another as they look for food.

Chapter 6

Long ago, there were huge flocks of wild turkeys. Some flocks were made up of thousands of turkeys. But wild turkeys became rare. Why did this happen?

People and Turkeys

Long ago, turkeys lived in most of the eastern and central parts of the United States. They lived north into parts of Canada, and south into Mexico. But settlers began to spread across America. They cut down the woods where turkeys lived to make farms. Settlers killed wild turkeys for food. By 1920, wild turkeys were rare. In many places where turkeys once lived, there were none left.

Once almost all of the world's turkeys lived on farms. There were few wild turkeys left alive.

There are places where wild turkeys are safe from people.
It is against the law to hunt turkeys in these places.

Luckily, some people cared about wild turkeys. These people made hunting laws. They set aside safe places where turkeys were protected. The numbers of turkeys grew. Some birds were caught and moved to places where all the turkeys had been killed off. After many years, turkeys were back in most of the places where they lived long ago. The wild turkey had been rescued.

Wild turkeys are no longer rare. Over one million wild turkeys live in the United States. Wild turkeys live in parts of Canada and Mexico, too.

On Sharing a Book

As you know, adults greatly influence a child's attitude toward reading. When a child sees you read, or when you share a book with a child, you're sending a message that reading is important. Show the child that reading a book together is important to you. Find a comfortable, quiet place. Turn off the television and limit other distractions, such as telephone calls.

  Be prepared to start slowly. Take turns reading parts of this book. Stop and talk about what you're reading. Talk about the photographs. You may find that much of the shared time is spent discussing just a few pages. This discussion time is valuable for both of you, so don't move through the book too quickly. If the child begins to lose interest, stop reading. Continue sharing the book at another time. When you do pick up the book again, be sure to revisit the parts you have already read. Most importantly, enjoy the book!

Be a Vocabulary Detective

You will find a word list on page 5. Words selected for this list are important to the understanding of the topic of this book. Encourage the child to be a word detective and search for the words as you read the book together. Talk about what the words mean and how they are used in the sentence. Do any of these words have more than one meaning? You will find these words defined in a glossary on page 46.

What about Questions?

Use questions to make sure the child understands the information in this book. Here are some suggestions:

> What did this paragraph tell us? What does this picture show? What do you think we'll learn about next? How are wild turkeys like domesticated turkeys? How are they different? Where do wild turkeys live? Could a wild turkey live in your backyard? Why/Why not? How big is a wild turkey? What do wild turkeys eat? What does a tom turkey do when he displays? How does a chick break out of its shell? What do you think it's like being a wild turkey? What is your favorite part of the book? Why?

If the child has questions, don't hesitate to respond with questions of your own such as: What do *you* think? Why? What is it that you don't know? If the child can't remember certain facts, turn to the index.

Introducing the Index

The index is an important learning tool. It helps readers get information quickly without searching throughout the whole book. Turn to the index on page 47. Choose an entry, such as *food,* and ask the child to use the index to find out what wild turkeys eat. Repeat this exercise with as many entries as you like. Ask the child to point out the differences between an index and a glossary. (The index helps readers find information quickly, while the glossary tells readers what words mean.)

All the World in Metric!

Although our monetary system is in metric units (based on multiples of 10), the United States is one of the few countries in the world that does not use the metric system of measurement. Here are some conversion activities you and the child can do using a calculator:

WHEN YOU KNOW:	MULTIPLY BY:	TO FIND:
miles	1.609	kilometers
feet	0.3048	meters
inches	2.54	centimeters
gallons	3.787	liters
tons	0.907	metric tons
pounds	0.454	kilograms

Activities

Make up a story about wild turkeys. Be sure to include information from this book. Draw or paint pictures to illustrate your story.

If a heavier bird and a lighter bird both have wings that are the same size, the heavier bird has to work harder to fly. You can do an experiment to show this. Make two paper airplanes out of tablet, typing, or computer paper. The two planes should be the same size and shape. Tape several coins to the top of one of the planes. Which plane flies better? Do you have to throw the weighted plane harder to make it fly? Does it matter if the coins are stacked or spread out? What happens if all of the coins are near the front or the back end of the plane? Repeat the experiment with different numbers of coins.

Glossary

beard—long, thin feathers growing from a male turkey's chest

displaying—showing off to try to attract females

domesticated (duh-MESS-tih-kay-tehd)—tamed to live with or be used by humans

down—soft, fluffy feathers

flock—a group of birds

gobblers—male turkeys

hens—female turkeys

incubating (ING-kyuh-bay-ting)—sitting on eggs and keeping them warm so they will hatch

poults (POHLTS)—young turkeys

predators (PREH-duh-turz)—animals who hunt other animals

roosting—resting in a tree for the night

snood—the loose piece of skin above a male turkey's beak

spurs—sharp spines on male turkeys' legs

toms—male turkeys

Index

Pages listed in **bold** type refer to photographs.

About the Author

Dorothy Hinshaw Patent was born in Minnesota and spent most of her growing-up years in Marin County, California. She has a Ph.D. in zoology from the University of California. She has great respect for the beauty and intelligence of wild turkeys. Dr. Patent is the author of over 100 nonfiction books for children including *Baby Horses, Dogs: The Wolf Within, Horses: Understanding Animals, Cattle: Understanding Animals,* and *Apple Trees.* Her books have received a number of awards, including the Golden Kite from the Society of Children's Book Writers and Illustrators and the Children's Choice Award from the International Reading Association. She has two grown sons and lives in Missoula, Montana, with her husband, Greg.

About the Photographer

William Muñoz lives with his wife and son in western Montana. He has been photographing nature for over 20 years. Mr. Muñoz exhibits his photographs at art fairs throughout the USA and has collaborated with Dorothy Patent on numerous critically acclaimed books for children.

10/07 Dents on cover